ARTIFICIAL INTELLIGENCE IN PROJECT MANAGEMENT

BY. ENG KHALED SABRE

Contents:

- About the Author 3
- Chapter 1: Introduction to Artificial Intelligence and Project Management 5
- Chapter 2: Fundamentals of Artificial Intelligence 8
- Chapter 3: Prompt Engineering 11
- Chapter 4: Applications of Artificial Intelligence in Project Management 16
- Chapter 5: Project Planning Using Artificial Intelligence .. 20
- Chapter Six: AI-Supported Decision Making 24
- Chapter Seven: Resource Management and Scheduling Using AI 27
- Chapter Eight: Risk Management and Prediction Using Artificial Intelligence 31
- Chapter Nine: Communication and Stakeholder Management Using Artificial Intelligence 35
- Chapter 10: Quality Assurance and Performance Management Using Artificial Intelligence 39
- Chapter 11: Challenges and Ethical Considerations in the Use of Artificial Intelligence 43
- Chapter 12: Implementing AI in Project Management 47
- Chapter 13: Case Studies and Practical Examples 51
- Chapter 14: The Future of Project Management with Artificial Intelligence 60
- Chapter 15: Conclusion and Recommendations 65
- Chapter 16: Sources 72

About the Author

Khaled AlSabaa: A Pioneer in Project Management and Generative AI

a leading figure in the field of project management and generative AI in Saudi Arabia. With over a decade of experience in mechanical engineering and project management, Khaled has successfully combined practical experience with theoretical knowledge in AI technologies and their applications in project management.

Qualifications and Certifications:

Holds a B.Sc. in Mechanical Engineering from the Arab Academy for Science and Technology.

Certified PMP® (Project Management Professional) and RMP® (Risk Management Professional) from the Project Management Institute (PMI).

Certified in "Data Landscape of GenAI for Project Managers" and "Generative AI Overview for Project Managers" from the Project Management Institute (PMI), where he learned essential concepts around data and generative AI models, including data types, quality, volume, and variety, as well as data governance, risks, and security threats.

Professional Experience:

Currently, Khaled works at Al-Fanar Projects, a leading company in managing large-scale projects in Saudi Arabia and the Middle East. he leads a multidisciplinary team in executing major projects, with a particular focus on integrating generative AI technologies into project management processes.

Achievements in AI:
During his tenure at Fanar Project, Khaled has developed and implemented several pioneering initiatives in using AI in projects

Vision and Objective:
Khaled believes that generative AI will play a central role in the future of project management. Through this book, he aims to provide a comprehensive and practical guide on how to leverage generative AI to enhance the efficiency and effectiveness of project management, with a focus on practical applications and real-world challenges faced by project managers in the Arab world.

Chapter 1: Introduction to Artificial Intelligence and Project Management

1.1 Definition of Artificial Intelligence

Artificial Intelligence (AI) is a field in computer science that focuses on creating intelligent systems capable of performing tasks that typically require human intelligence. According to the reference documents, AI can be more specifically defined as the ability of machines to:

- Perceive and understand their environment.
- Learn from instruction, training, and their own experiences.
- Make decisions based on stored memories and thinking processes.
- Conduct natural conversations and linguistic communication with humans.
- Develop "intuition" in ambiguous and imprecise situations.

This comprehensive definition highlights the three main elements of AI: perception, prediction, and planning. These capabilities enable AI systems to simulate and enhance human abilities in a wide range of tasks and applications.

1.2 Importance of AI in Project Management

AI plays an increasingly key role in the field of project management, offering many benefits that can significantly improve the efficiency and effectiveness of project management processes:

1. Automation of routine tasks: AI can handle repetitive and time-consuming tasks, freeing up project managers' time to focus on strategic aspects of the project.

2. Improving the accuracy of estimates and predictions: By analyzing historical data and current project trends, AI systems can provide more accurate estimates for costs, timelines, and required resources.
3. Enhancing decision-making: AI can quickly analyze vast amounts of data and provide data-driven insights to support informed decision-making.
4. Improving risk management: By identifying patterns and analyzing historical data, AI systems can help predict potential risks and suggest mitigation strategies.
5. Increasing efficiency in communication and stakeholder management: AI can assist in personalizing communication, analyzing feedback, and improving collaboration between team members and stakeholders.

1.3 Overview of the Report Content

This report provides a comprehensive overview of the use of AI in project management, covering the following topics:

- Fundamentals of AI and its applications in project management: Explaining the basic concepts of AI and how they apply in the context of project management.
- Prompt engineering techniques and their importance: Exploring the importance of formulating effective prompts when using generative AI tools.
- - How to use AI in various aspects of project management: Providing concrete examples of how to integrate AI into distinct phases and processes of project management.
- Challenges and ethical considerations: Discussing ethical issues and challenges associated with using AI in project management.
- Case studies and practical examples: Presenting real-world examples of how organizations have benefited from AI in managing their projects.

- Outlook for project management with AI: Exploring future trends and how AI will continue to shape the future of project management.

Through this comprehensive content, the report aims to provide project managers and professionals with a deep understanding of the potential of AI in improving project management practices and enhancing project outcomes.

Chapter 2: Fundamentals of Artificial Intelligence

2.1 Types of Artificial Intelligence

AI can be classified into two main types based on the nature of outputs and applications:

1- Generative AI:
- Focuses on creating new and innovative content.
- Uses machine learning techniques to produce texts, images, videos, or any other type of data.
- Examples include ChatGPT for text generation and DALL-E for image generation.
- Relies on large language models (LLMs) trained on vast amounts of data.

2- Analytical or Predictive AI
- Focuses on understanding and analyzing existing data and predicting future outcomes.
- Used in pattern analysis, decision-making, and predicting future trends.
- Applications include customer behavior prediction, project risk analysis, and financial performance forecasting.

2.2 Foundation Models and Large Language Models

Foundation Models:
- Are large pre-trained models on vast amounts of unlabeled data.
- Used as a basis for multiple AI tasks.
- Can be adapted for specific tasks through additional training on relevant data.

Large Language Models (LLMs):
- Are a type of foundation model specifically designed for natural language understanding and generation.

- Definition: Deep neural models trained on massive amounts of text to understand and produce human language

How they work:
- Learn language patterns by analyzing millions of texts.
- Use the "Attention" technique to understand context and word relationships.
- Generate new texts based on learned patterns.

Their importance:
- Enable complex linguistic tasks such as translation, text summarization, and content creation.
- Contribute to the development of intelligent applications such as virtual assistants and chatbots.

2.3 The Seven Patterns of AI in Projects

Hyper-Personalization:
1. Using machine learning to develop a profile for each individual and customize services and content according to their preferences.
   Example: Personalizing product recommendations or content for each user in a digital platform development project.
2. Goal-Driven Systems:
   Enabling AI to learn by achieving specific goals.
   Example: Using AI to optimize project scheduling to achieve specific time objectives.
3. Pattern and Anomaly Detection:
   Using machine learning to identify unusual or anomalous patterns in data and processes.
   Example: Discovering potential project risks by analyzing data from previous projects.
4. Recognition:
   Identifying and classifying images, video, audio, and objects.
   Example: Using image recognition techniques to analyze construction progress in building projects.
5. Predictive Analytics:
   Using historical data to predict future outcomes.

Example: Predicting project costs and timeline based on previous project data.
6. Continuous Learning:
Continuously improving system performance through learning from new data and interactions.
Example: Continuously improving project risk management models with each new project.
7. Intelligent Automation:
Automating complex tasks and processes using AI.
Example: Automating the process of preparing reports and project status updates.

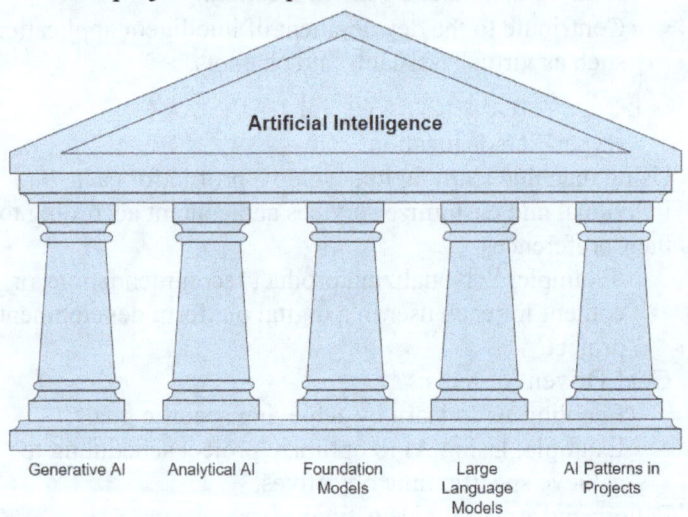

These seven patterns provide a comprehensive framework for understanding how AI can be applied in project management, helping organizations identify appropriate opportunities to use AI to improve the efficiency and effectiveness of project management.

Chapter 3: Prompt Engineering

3.1 Definition of Prompt Engineering

Prompt engineering is the process of designing and optimizing natural language inputs to obtain specific results from generative AI systems. According to the Massachusetts Institute of Technology (MIT), "Prompts are your inputs to the AI system to get specific results. In other words, prompts are the beginnings of the conversation: what you tell the AI and how you tell it to get useful responses for you."

Prompt engineering is considered a fundamental digital skill in the age of generative AI, enabling users to interact effectively with AI systems and guide them to produce the required outputs accurately.

3.2 Importance of Effective Prompts

The importance of effective prompts lies in several aspects:

1. Improving the accuracy and relevance of outputs:
   - Good prompts help guide large language models (LLMs) to produce more accurate and relevant results.
   - They reduce the likelihood of getting irrelevant or inaccurate answers.
2. Increasing the efficiency of using AI tools:
   - They enable users to obtain the required information more quickly.
   - They reduce the need to repeat questions or rephrase them.
3. Enabling users to obtain more useful and customized results:
   - They allow for directing AI to meet specific and specialized needs.
   - They help extract complex or specialized information more effectively.

According to a study conducted by BCG, about 90% of participants, regardless of their baseline proficiency level, produced higher quality results when using GPT-4 for tasks,

==confirming the importance of effective prompts in improving performance.==

3.3 Strategies and Techniques for Writing Prompts

To write effective prompts, the following strategies and techniques can be used:

1. Using the "divergence and convergence" approach:
   - Start with a broad, open-ended question to explore possibilities.
   - Then gradually focus on the most important points.
2. Providing more context than you would give to a human:
   - Provide ample background information about the topic.
   - Clarify the purpose of the question and the intended use of the answer.
3. Giving examples:
   - Include specific examples in the text to illustrate the form or type of answer required.
   - This helps in obtaining more accurate and relevant answers.
4. Making it a conversation, not a command:
   - Interact with AI as if it were a trainee who needs continuous guidance.
   - Ask follow-up questions and modify prompts based on responses.
5. Incorporating a "reliability check":
   - Request references and sources in the question.
   - This helps in assessing the accuracy and reliability of the information provided.

3.4 Prompt Patterns

There are several prompt patterns that can be used to improve interaction with AI systems:

1. Persona:
    - Make the AI act as an expert in a specific field.
    - Example: "Act as an experienced project manager in the software industry..."
2. Flipped interaction:
    - Make the AI ask questions instead of answering them.
    - Useful for discovering new aspects of the problem.
3. Alternative approach:
    - Request diverse ways to solve a problem or implement a task.
    - Helps explore creative solutions.
4. Question refinement:
    - Improve the questions asked to get more accurate answers.
5. Cognitive verifier:
    - Request an explanation of the logic behind the answers provided.
6. Fact checklist:
    - Request a list of facts related to a specific topic.
7. Reflection:
    - Request analysis and evaluation of previous answers.

3.5 Prompting Techniques

There are three main prompting techniques:

1. Zero-shot prompts:

- Ask a direct question without providing additional examples or context.
- Suitable for simple and straightforward questions.

2. Few-shot prompts:

- Provide some examples or context before asking the main question.
- Help guide AI towards the required pattern of answers.

3. Chain-of-thought prompts:

- Break down the complex problem into sequential steps or thoughts.
- Help in obtaining more detailed and logical answers.

Refining AI Interactions through Prompt Engineering

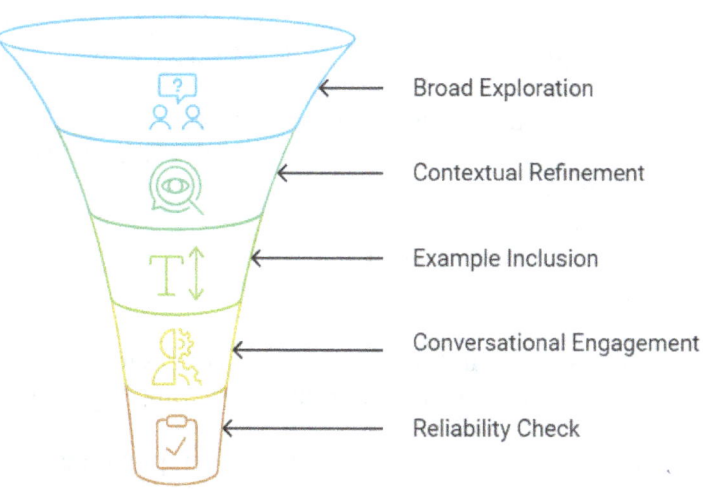

By understanding and applying these strategies and techniques, project managers can improve their interaction with AI systems and obtain more useful and effective results in managing their projects.

Chapter 4: Applications of Artificial Intelligence in Project Management

4.1 Automation in Project Management Tasks

AI can automate many routine tasks in project management, saving time and effort for project managers and increasing efficiency:

1. Creating and summarizing common project management documents:

   - AI can create initial drafts for project documents such as the project charter and project management plan.
   - It can automatically summarize long reports and documents to extract key points.

2. Automating periodic reports and status updates:

   - Generate project status reports periodically using updated data.
   - Produce automated updates for stakeholders on project progress.

3. Automatic task scheduling and resource allocation:

   - Use AI algorithms to create optimal project schedules.
   - Dynamically allocate resources based on team skills and resource availability.

4.2 Assistance in Decision Making

AI can support the decision-making process in project management through:

1. Analyzing big data to extract valuable insights:

   - Analyze historical data from previous projects to identify success and failure factors.
   - Extract patterns and trends from current project data to predict potential problems.

2. Providing data-driven recommendations for problem-solving:

   - Suggest solutions to problems based on analysis of similar cases in previous projects.
   - Provide multiple options for problem-solving with an assessment of pros and cons for each option.

3. Supporting risk assessment and identifying appropriate strategies:

   - Analyze potential risks using predictive models.
   - Suggest risk mitigation strategies based on their effectiveness in similar projects.

4.3 Enhancing Analytical Capabilities

AI can enhance the analytical capabilities of project managers through:

1. Improving the accuracy of estimates and predictions:

   - Use machine learning to improve cost and time estimates based on historical data.

- Predict future project trends using advanced forecasting models.

2. Analyzing project performance and identifying areas for improvement:

- Continuously analyze key performance indicators (KPIs) to identify deviations.
- Identify areas for improvement in processes and performance using machine learning techniques.

3. Providing in-depth insights into project and industry trends:

- Analyze external data to understand industry trends and their impact on the project.
- Provide competitive analyses to compare project performance with industry benchmarks.

4.4 Improving Communication and Stakeholder Management

AI can help improve communication and stakeholder management through:

1. Personalizing communication based on stakeholder preferences:

- Analyze communication preferences for each stakeholder and customize messages accordingly.
- Suggest the best channels and times to communicate with each stakeholder.

2. Analyzing feedback and adapting communication strategies:

- Use sentiment analysis to understand stakeholder reactions to project updates.
- Modify communication strategies based on continuous feedback.

3. Facilitating effective collaboration between team members:

   - Use AI tools to improve communication and collaboration across geographically distributed teams.
   - Analyze interaction patterns between team members to identify opportunities for improving collaboration.

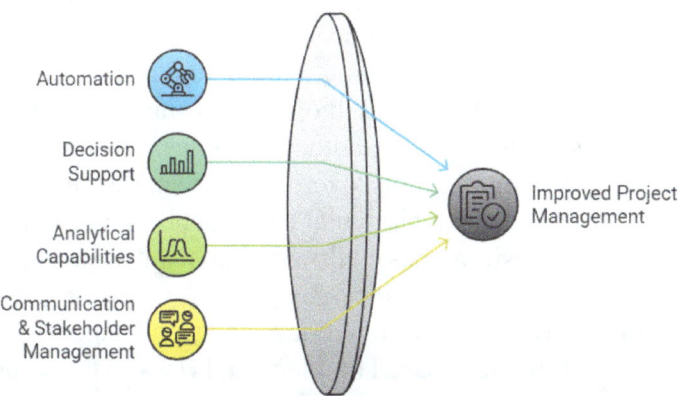

AI-Enhanced Project Management

Through these applications, AI can help project managers improve the efficiency and effectiveness of project management, leading to increased project success rates and better outcomes for organizations.

Chapter 5: Project Planning Using Artificial Intelligence

5.1 Prioritization and Risk Management

- Using AI to analyze and prioritize tasks: AI can analyze historical data from previous projects and identify key factors that affect task success. Using this information, the system can rank tasks according to importance and impact on the overall project. For example, the system can identify critical tasks that have a significant impact on the schedule or budget and give them high priority.
- Identifying potential risks using predictive analytics: AI can use machine learning models to analyze data from past and current projects to identify risk patterns. The system can predict potential risks based on factors such as project type, size, industry, and other variables. For instance, the system might discover that software development projects in a particular sector tend to face delays in the testing phase, allowing the team to prepare for this risk in advance.
- Developing initiative-taking risk management strategies: Based on identified risks, AI can suggest strategies to mitigate these risks. The system can analyze the effectiveness of different mitigation strategies in previous projects and suggest the most successful ones. For example, if there is a risk of delayed delivery from a supplier, the system might suggest strategies such as including penalty clauses in the contract or searching for alternative suppliers.

5.2 Resource Allocation and Task Scheduling

- Optimizing resource allocation using AI algorithms: AI can analyze team members' skills and experiences, resource availability, and project requirements to determine the optimal resource allocation. The system can consider factors such as skill level, previous experience, and current workload of each team member to ensure effective task distribution.
- Creating dynamic schedules that adapt to project changes: AI can create flexible schedules that consider changes in the project and available resources. The system can automatically update the schedule when changes occur, such as a task delay or availability of additional resources, considering the impact of these changes on the project.
- Automatically identifying and resolving resource conflicts: AI can identify resource conflict situations, such as allocating the same resource to two simultaneous tasks and suggesting solutions. This may include rescheduling tasks, allocating alternative resources, or suggesting modifications to the project scope to avoid conflicts.

5.3 Creating Business Use Cases

- Using AI to analyze market data and trends: AI can collect and analyze copious amounts of market data, including industry trends, consumer behavior, and competitor performance. The system can use this information to identify potential opportunities and threats for the project.

- Generating multiple scenarios to evaluate project feasibility: Using simulation models, AI can create multiple scenarios to assess project feasibility under different conditions. The system can evaluate the impact of variables such as market changes, variable costs, or regulatory changes on project success.
- Providing data-driven recommendations to improve project value: Based on data analysis and different scenarios, AI can provide recommendations to improve project value. This may include suggestions for modifying project scope, targeting specific markets, or changing pricing strategies.

5.4 Improving Cost and Timeline Estimation

- Using historical data to improve estimation accuracy: AI can analyze data from previous projects to identify factors that affect estimation accuracy. Using this information, the system can create more accurate predictive models for costs and timelines for new projects.
- Identifying factors affecting costs and timelines: AI can analyze a wide range of factors that may impact costs and timelines, such as project complexity, team size, changes in material prices, and others. The system can determine the importance of each factor and how it affects the estimates.
- Providing real-time updates to estimates based on project progress: AI can continuously monitor project progress and update estimates in real-time. If changes or delays occur, the system can automatically adjust estimates and alert the project team to potential changes in costs or timelines.

By using these advanced AI techniques in project planning, project managers can improve planning accuracy, increase resource utilization efficiency, and enhance the ability to predict and manage risks. This, in turn, leads to increased chances of project success and more effective achievement of objectives.

Chapter Six: AI-Supported Decision Making

6.1 Big Data Analysis

• Using machine learning techniques to analyze vast amounts of project data:

- AI can process and analyze huge quantities of data faster and more efficiently than humans.
- Utilizing machine learning algorithms such as deep learning and reinforcement learning to discover complex patterns and relationships in data.
- Analyzing historical data from previous projects to extract lessons learned and identify success factors.

• Extracting valuable insights from diverse data sources:

- Integrating data from multiple sources such as project reports, performance records, customer data, and market data.
- Using data mining techniques to discover valuable and hidden information in these diverse data sets.
- Transforming raw data into actionable information that can be used in decision-making.

• Identifying non-obvious trends and patterns in project data:

- Using predictive analytics techniques to discover potential future trends in the project.
- Identifying non-obvious patterns that may indicate potential opportunities or risks.
- Using anomaly analysis techniques to detect any unusual deviations from expected patterns.

6.2 Predicting Project Outcomes

• Using prediction models to forecast potential project outcomes:

- Building predictive models using historical and current project data.
- Using techniques such as time series analysis and regression to predict key project performance indicators.
- Creating multiple scenarios for potential project outcomes based on different inputs.

• Identifying key factors influencing project success:

- Using correlation and regression analysis to determine the factors most influencing project success.
- Analyzing the importance of different variables in prediction models to understand their relative impact.
- Using machine learning techniques such as decision trees to identify critical factors in project success.

• Providing early warnings for potential problems:

- Creating AI-based early warning systems to detect early indicators of potential problems.
- Using machine learning techniques to analyze real-time data and detect deviations from the plan.
- Sending automated alerts to the project team when potential risks are detected.

6.3 Improving Decision Quality

• Improving Decision Quality:

- Using AI to analyze historical and current data and provide evidence-based recommendations.
- Developing decision support systems that combine human expertise with AI capabilities.
- Presenting multiple decision options with analysis of pros and cons for each option.

• Analyzing different scenarios and evaluating their impacts:

- Using simulation techniques to create and analyze different project scenarios.
- Assessing the impact of different decisions on key project performance indicators.
- Using sensitivity analysis to understand how changes in inputs affect project outcomes.

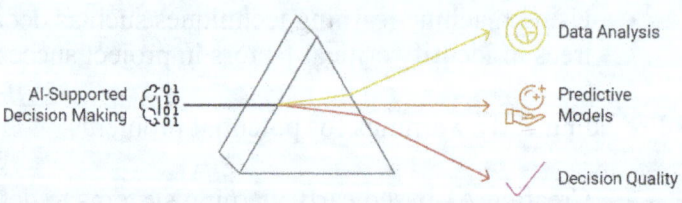

By using these advanced AI techniques in decision-making, project managers can improve the accuracy and effectiveness of their decisions, leading to increased chances of project success and more efficient achievement of objectives.

Chapter Seven: Resource Management and Scheduling Using AI

7.1 Optimizing Resource Allocation

AI can play a pivotal role in improving the resource allocation process in project management through: Using AI to analyze team members' skills and capabilities:

- Developing machine learning models to analyze resumes and past performance records of team members.
- Identifying strengths and weaknesses of each team member based on historical data analysis.
- Creating accurate skill and experience profiles for each team member.

• Determining the best resource allocation based on project requirements and timelines:

- Using optimization algorithms to match employee skills with task requirements.
- Considering factors such as resource availability, cost, and timelines when allocating resources.
- Identifying the optimal resource allocation that balances efficiency and effectiveness.

• Predicting future resource needs and capacity planning:

- Using forecasting models to predict future resource needs based on project trends and historical data.
- Identifying potential skill or capacity gaps before they occur.

- Developing initiative-taking plans for skill development or hiring additional resources as needed.

7.2 Dynamic Project Scheduling

AI can improve the project scheduling process through:

• Creating flexible schedules that adapt to project changes:

- Using dynamic scheduling algorithms that can adapt to changes in project scope or resources.
- Incorporating uncertainty and risk factors into scheduling models to create more realistic timelines.
- Providing multiple schedule options with analysis of pros and cons for each option.

• Updating schedules in real-time based on progress and changes:

- Using real-time monitoring systems to track project progress and automatically update schedules.
- Analyzing the impact of changes or delays on the overall project timeline.
- Suggesting schedule adjustments to compensate for delays or accommodation changes.

• Optimizing task sequencing to minimize overall project time:

- Using optimization algorithms to determine the optimal sequence of tasks.
- Analyzing dependencies between tasks and identifying opportunities for parallel task execution.

- Suggesting task reordering to minimize overall project time while considering constraints and available resources.

7.3 Constraint and Dependency Management

AI can help manage constraints and dependencies more effectively by:

• Identifying and analyzing constraints and dependencies between tasks and resources:

- Using network analysis techniques to identify complex relationships between tasks and resources.
- Developing mathematical models to accurately represent constraints and dependencies.
- Analyzing the impact of constraints on schedule, cost, and quality.

• Suggesting solutions to mitigate the impact of constraints on the schedule:

- Using optimization techniques to suggest alternatives to mitigate the impact of constraints.
- Providing multiple scenarios for solving constraint problems with risk and benefit analysis for each scenario.
- Suggesting strategies for reallocating resources or rescheduling tasks to overcome constraints.

• Improving project critical path management:

- Using AI to accurately identify and analyze the critical path.

- Dynamically updating the critical path as the project progresses and conditions change.
- Suggesting strategies to shorten the critical path and accelerate project completion.

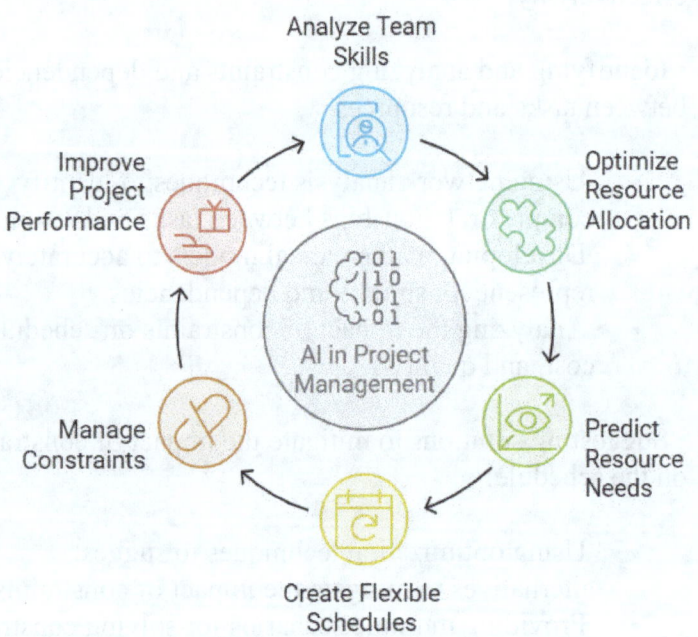

AI-Driven Project Management Cycle

By using these advanced AI techniques in resource management and scheduling, project managers can improve resource utilization efficiency, increase schedule flexibility, and better handle complex constraints and dependencies. This, in turn, leads to improved project performance and increased chances of success in achieving its objectives within the specified time and budget.

Chapter Eight: Risk Management and Prediction Using Artificial Intelligence

8.1 Identifying Potential Risks

Artificial intelligence can play a crucial role in identifying potential project risks more accurately and comprehensively:

• Using machine learning techniques to analyze data from previous projects and identify risk patterns:

- Analyzing historical data from past projects to discover patterns and relationships associated with risks.
- Using machine learning algorithms such as deep learning to identify hidden factors that may lead to risks.
- Creating predictive models that can recognize potential risk indicators in new projects.

• Predicting potential risks based on current project characteristics:

- Analyzing current project characteristics such as size, complexity, industry, and geographic location.
- Comparing these characteristics with previous projects to identify similar potential risks.
- Using predictive analysis techniques to forecast future risks based on current trends.

• Creating a comprehensive and continuously updated risk register:

- Automating the process of updating the risk register using AI to ensure real-time updates.
- Integrating data from multiple sources to create a comprehensive picture of potential risks.
- Using natural language processing techniques to analyze reports and documents to extract risk information.

8.2 Scenario Analysis and Impact Assessment

AI can improve the process of scenario analysis and risk impact assessment:

• Using simulation models to assess the impact of different risks on the project:

- Creating complex simulation models that consider many variables and interactions.
- Running thousands of scenarios in a brief time to understand the range of potential impacts.
- Updating simulation models in real-time as project conditions change.

• Analyzing multiple scenarios to understand potential outcomes:

- Using advanced statistical analysis techniques to evaluate the probability and impact of different scenarios.
- Identifying key factors that affect the outcomes of each scenario.
- Creating visual representations of different scenarios to facilitate understanding and decision-making.

• Providing data-driven recommendations for risk-related decisions:

- Using decision-making algorithms to provide objective recommendations based on data analysis.
- Providing cost-benefit analysis for different mitigation strategies.
- Using reinforcement learning techniques to improve the quality of recommendations over time.

8.3 Risk Mitigation Strategies

AI can assist in developing and implementing effective risk mitigation strategies:

• Suggesting effective risk mitigation strategies based on data analysis:

- Analyzing the effectiveness of previous mitigation strategies in similar projects.
- Using machine learning techniques to identify the most effective strategies for each type of risk.
- Creating customized mitigation strategies based on unique project characteristics.

• Prioritizing mitigation strategies based on their expected effectiveness:

- Using prediction models to estimate the effectiveness of each mitigation strategy.
- Analyzing the cost and benefit of each strategy to determine the best use of resources.
- Creating an optimal schedule for implementing mitigation strategies based on priority and available resources.

• Monitoring the effectiveness of mitigation strategies and adjusting them as needed:

- Using real-time monitoring systems to track the effectiveness of mitigation strategies.
- Applying machine learning techniques to identify deviations from expected performance.
- Suggesting adjustments to mitigation strategies based on actual data and changing conditions.

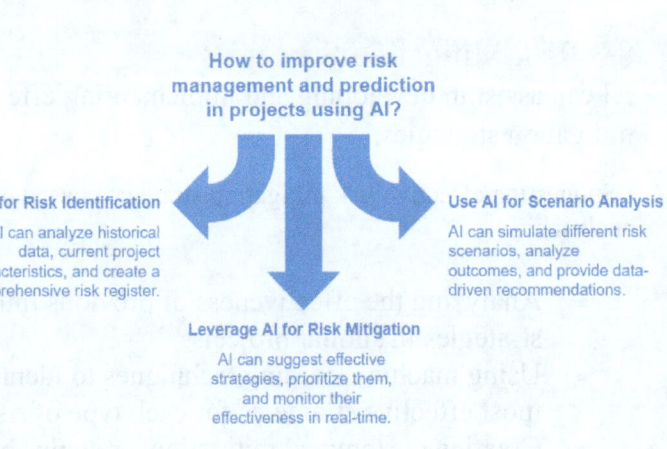

By using these advanced AI techniques in risk management and prediction, project managers can improve their ability to anticipate potential risks and respond to them effectively. This leads to increased likelihood of project success and reduced negative impacts of unexpected risks.

Chapter Nine: Communication and Stakeholder Management Using Artificial Intelligence

9.1 Improving Team Communication

Artificial Intelligence can play a key role in improving communication within the project team through:

• Using AI to analyze communication patterns and identify improvement opportunities:

- Analyzing email logs, instant messages, and conversations to identify communication patterns.
- Discovering communication gaps or areas that need improvement.
- Providing recommendations to improve the efficiency and effectiveness of team communication.

• Automating the creation and distribution of reports and updates:

- Automatically generating project status reports using updated data.
- Scheduling and sending periodic updates to team members and stakeholders.
- Customizing report content and format based on recipient needs.

• Personalizing communication based on team member preferences:

- Analyzing communication preferences for each team member (such as preferred communication methods and times).
- Adapting message style and content to suit each team member.
- Suggesting the best times and channels to communicate with each member to ensure maximum impact.

9.2 Managing Stakeholder Expectations

AI can help manage stakeholder expectations more effectively by:

• Analyzing stakeholder interests and expectations using natural language processing techniques:

- Analyzing documents and correspondence to understand stakeholder interests and priorities.
- Extracting key words and phrases that indicate specific expectations.
- Creating detailed profiles for each stakeholder including their interests and expectations.

• Predicting stakeholder reactions to project decisions and changes:

- Using machine learning models to predict how stakeholders will respond to proposed changes.
- Identifying potential risks associated with stakeholder reactions.
- Suggesting strategies to mitigate risks and proactively manage expectations.

- Developing customized communication strategies for each stakeholder group:

  - Classifying stakeholders into groups based on their interests and influence on the project.
  - Creating customized messages that align with the needs and expectations of each group.
  - Suggesting the most effective communication channels and methods for each group.

9.3 Analyzing Feedback and Adapting Strategies

AI can assist in analyzing feedback and adapting communication strategies by:

- Collecting and analyzing stakeholder feedback using sentiment analysis techniques:

  - Using natural language processing techniques to analyze comments and feedback.
  - Identifying positive and negative sentiments and opinions towards various aspects of the project.
  - Measuring stakeholder satisfaction levels and tracking changes over time.

- Identifying emerging trends and issues through data analysis:

  - Using machine learning techniques to discover patterns and trends in stakeholder feedback.
  - Identifying recurring or escalating issues that may need immediate attention.
  - Anticipating potential problems before they become key issues.

• Modifying communication and stakeholder management strategies based on analytics:

- Suggesting adjustments to communication plans based on ongoing feedback.
- Updating stakeholder profiles and adapting strategies accordingly.
- Providing real-time recommendations to improve communication and relationship management with stakeholders.

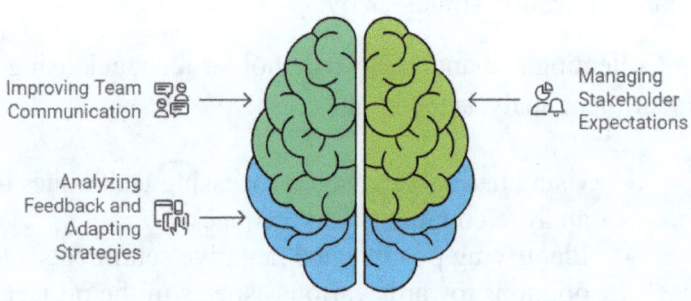

By using these advanced AI techniques in communication and stakeholder management, project managers can improve the effectiveness of team communication, better manage stakeholder expectations, and respond quickly to changes in stakeholder needs and opinions. This, in turn, leads to increased stakeholder satisfaction and improved chances of project success.

Chapter 10: Quality Assurance and Performance Management Using Artificial Intelligence

10.1 Real-Time Project Quality Monitoring

Artificial intelligence can play a crucial role in continuously monitoring project quality in real time:

- Using AI systems to monitor key quality indicators:

  - Developing machine learning models to analyze data streaming from various project sources.
  - Creating smart dashboards that display key performance indicators (KPIs) in real time.
  - Integrating data from different systems to provide a comprehensive view of project quality.

- Quickly identifying deviations from established quality standards:

  - Utilizing anomaly detection algorithms to identify any deviations from expected quality standards.
  - Establish an early warning system that alerts the project team immediately upon detecting any quality issues.
  - Analyzing historical patterns to predict potential problems before they occur.

- Automating inspection and quality assurance processes:

  - Employing computer vision techniques to automate visual inspection processes of products or outputs.
  - Developing bots to conduct routine quality tests on software or systems.

- Automating the collection and analysis of quality data to provide accurate and timely reports.

10.2 Performance Analysis and Improvement Areas Identification

AI can assist in deeply analyzing project performance and identifying improvement opportunities:
- Analyzing project performance data to identify trends and patterns:

  - Utilizing deep learning techniques to analyze large volumes of project data.
  - Identifying obscure relationships between various aspects of project performance.
  - Creating advanced data visualizations to facilitate understanding of complex trends and patterns.
- Comparing current project performance with previous projects and industry standards:

  - Developing machine learning models for automatic comparisons between the current project and past projects.
  - Integrating data from external sources to compare project performance with industry benchmarks.
  - Identifying areas where the project excels or falls short of expected standards.
- Providing recommendations for performance improvement based on analyses:

  - Using AI to generate specific recommendations for enhancing project performance.
  - Developing predictive models to assess the impact of proposed changes on project performance.

- Creating tailored action plans to address identified weaknesses in project performance.

10.3 Continuous Learning and Process Improvement

AI can assist in continuous learning and improving project management processes:

- Using machine learning techniques to analyze lessons learned from previous projects:

  - Developing natural language processing models to analyze post-project reports and lessons learned.
  - Identifying patterns and trends in successes and challenges across multiple projects.
  - Creating a dynamic knowledge base that continuously updates with new experiences.

- Identifying and applying best practices to current and future projects:

  - Using reinforcement learning techniques to identify the most effective strategies in project management.
  - Developing smart recommendation systems to suggest best practices based on the characteristics of the current project.
  - Automating the integration of lessons learned into project management methodologies and tools.

- Developing predictive models to enhance planning and execution of future projects:

  - Utilizing deep learning techniques to build accurate predictive models for various aspects of project performance.

- Integrating data from multiple sources to improve the accuracy of predictions.
- Developing advanced simulation tools to test different project scenarios before execution.

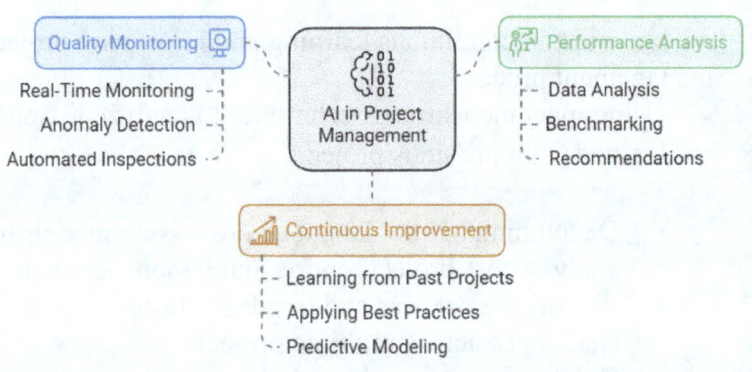

By employing these advanced AI techniques in quality assurance and performance management, project managers can significantly enhance project quality, quickly identify areas for improvement, and ensure continuous learning and process enhancement. This, in turn, leads to increased project success rates and better outcomes for organizations.

Chapter 11: Challenges and Ethical Considerations in the Use of Artificial Intelligence

11.1 Data Protection and Privacy

As the use of AI in project management increases, protecting data and privacy becomes critical:

- Identifying data security risks when using AI systems:
  - Conducting regular risk assessments to identify potential vulnerabilities in AI systems.
  - Analyzing data flows to understand how data is collected, processed, and stored.
  - Identifying sensitive data types that may be at risk in case of a breach.
- Implementing best practices for protecting personal and sensitive data:
  - Employing strong encryption techniques to protect data in transit and at rest.
  - Using anonymization and data masking techniques to safeguard personal information.
  - Applying the principle of least privilege to ensure restricted access to sensitive data.
- Compliance with local and global data protection regulations:
  - Understanding and applying requirements of regulations like GDPR, CCPA, and other local laws.
  - Establishing clear policies and procedures for handling personal data.
  - Conducting regular audits to ensure ongoing compliance with data protection regulations.

11.2 Algorithmic Bias and How to Address It

Bias in AI systems can lead to unfair decisions in project management:
- Understanding sources of bias in AI systems:

  - Identifying potential biases in the training data used to build AI models.
  - Examining how human assumptions and decisions in algorithm design affect outcomes.
  - Analyzing the impact of cultural and social contexts on data interpretation and decision-making.
- Developing strategies to detect and mitigate bias in models and algorithms:

  - Using advanced tools and techniques to test models for potential biases.
  - Applying fair machine learning techniques to reduce bias in decision-making processes.
  - Conducting regular reviews of AI outputs to check for bias patterns.
- Ensuring fairness and equity in AI use in project management:

  - Establishing clear standards for fairness and equity in AI applications.
  - Diversifying AI development teams to ensure representation of diverse perspectives.
  - Creating mechanisms for feedback and correction when inequities are identified.

11.3 Transparency and Accountability in Decision-Making

Ensuring transparency and accountability in AI use is essential for building trust and ensuring responsible use:

- Developing mechanisms to clearly explain AI decisions:

  - Utilizing explainable AI (XAI) techniques to clarify how decisions are made.
  - Creating user-friendly interfaces to display the logic behind AI-driven decisions.
  - Providing detailed explanations for significant or controversial decisions.
- Ensuring appropriate human oversight on critical decisions:

  - Identifying areas that require human review and approval before implementing AI decisions.
  - Establishing processes for human intervention when necessary to correct or modify AI decisions.
  - Training staff to critically understand and evaluate AI system outputs.
- Creating an accountability framework for AI use in project management:

  - Defining clear roles and responsibilities for all participants in the development and use of AI systems.
  - Establishing mechanisms for reporting concerns and issues related to AI use.
  - Developing policies and procedures for addressing misuse or failure of AI.

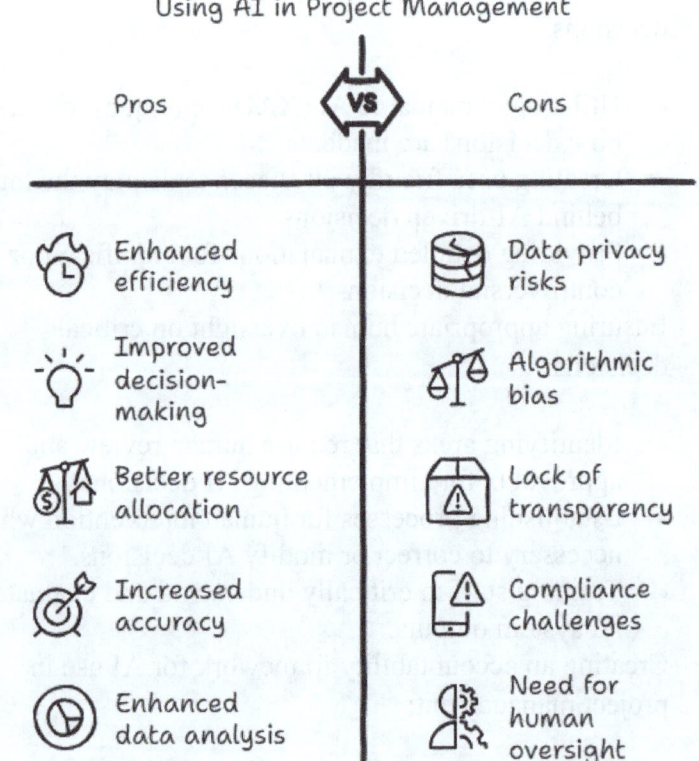

By addressing these challenges and ethical considerations, project managers can ensure the responsible and ethical use of AI. This not only helps avoid legal and reputational risks but also contributes to building trust with stakeholders and enhancing the acceptance and adoption of AI technologies in project management.

Chapter 12: Implementing AI in Project Management

12.1 Assessing Organizational Readiness

Assessing organizational readiness is a crucial step before implementing AI in project management. This includes:

- Analyzing current technological infrastructure and its suitability for AI applications:

  - Conducting a comprehensive audit of existing systems, software, and hardware.
  - Identifying necessary updates or upgrades to support AI applications.
  - Evaluating current data storage and processing capabilities for AI adequacy.

- Assessing employee skills and capabilities in AI:

  - Conducting a skills assessment to determine employees' knowledge level of AI.
  - Identifying internal experts who can lead AI initiatives.
  - Evaluating employees' readiness to adopt AI technologies in their daily work.

- Identifying gaps and needs for successful AI implementation:

  - Analyzing the gap between status and future AI requirements.
  - Identifying additional resources needed, whether technological or human.
  - Developing a plan to bridge these gaps, including budget and timeline considerations.

12.2 Choosing the Right Tools and Technologies

Selecting the appropriate tools and technologies is critical to ensure the success of AI implementation:

- Reviewing and evaluating available market solutions:

    - Conducting thorough research on AI tools and technologies available for project management.
    - Evaluating the pros and cons of each solution, considering cost, performance, and ease of use.
    - Requesting demos or trial versions from vendors to assess tools.

- Identifying tools and technologies that align with organizational needs and goals:

    - Matching tool features with the specific project management needs of the organization.
    - Considering scalability and flexibility to meet future requirements.
    - Evaluating tool compatibility with the existing organizational culture and workflows.

- Developing a plan for integrating selected tools with current systems:

    - Identifying integration points with existing systems like project management tools and databases.
    - Creating a timeline for phased implementation to minimize disruptions to ongoing operations.
    - Developing a strategy for data migration and ensuring compatibility with legacy systems.

12.3 Training the Team and Change Management

The success of AI implementation heavily relies on effective team training and change management:

- Developing comprehensive training programs to enhance team skills in using AI:

  - Designing tailored training courses covering the fundamentals of AI and its applications in project management.
  - Providing firsthand training on new tools and technologies.
  - Creating personalized learning paths for distinct roles within the project team.
- Managing the cultural and organizational change associated with AI adoption:

  - Developing a clear communication strategy to explain the benefits and impact of AI on daily operations.
  - Involving team leaders and key stakeholders as change ambassadors.
  - Proactively addressing concerns and resistance through open dialogue and transparency.
- Establishing mechanisms for continuous learning and knowledge sharing on best practices:

  - Creating communities of practice for sharing experiences and lessons learned.
  - Organizing regular knowledge-sharing sessions and highlighting successful case studies.
  - Encouraging a culture of experimentation and learning from mistakes in using AI technologies.

Implementing AI in Project Management

| Assess Organizational Readiness | Choose Right Tools and Technologies | Train Team and Manage Change |

By following these steps, organizations can implement AI in project management in a structured and effective manner, ensuring they are technically and humanly prepared to adopt this transformative technology. Careful readiness assessment, appropriate tool selection, and a focus on team training and change management are all critical factors for the successful implementation of AI in project management.

Chapter 13: Case Studies and Practical Examples

13.1 Successes in Applying AI in Project Management

- <u>Case Study 1: Using AI to Improve Project Scheduling in a Major Tech Company</u>

Background:
A major tech company faced challenges in project scheduling and resource allocation, leading to project delays and budget overruns. The company relied on fixed scheduling templates that did not account for the unique complexities and variables of each project.

AI Application:
The company decided to integrate an AI-powered project management tool that utilized machine learning to enhance scheduling processes. By inputting the project scope and expected duration, the tool generated a detailed Work Breakdown Structure (WBS) and an optimized timeline. It leveraged historical data and contextual information to create customized schedules for each project.

Results:

- **Time Savings:** Reduced the time spent on creating schedules significantly, allowing project managers to focus on strategic aspects.
- **Improved Accuracy:** Enhanced the accuracy of schedules and forecasts, leading to fewer delays and budget overruns.

- **Resource Allocation Optimization:** Enhanced the allocation of human and physical resources, increasing operational efficiency.

Lessons Learned:

- **Automating Routine Processes:** AI can take over repetitive tasks, saving time and effort.
- **Leveraging Historical Data:** Utilizing past data improves project estimates and planning.
- **Enhancing Planning Accuracy:** AI can improve schedule accuracy, supporting better decision-making.

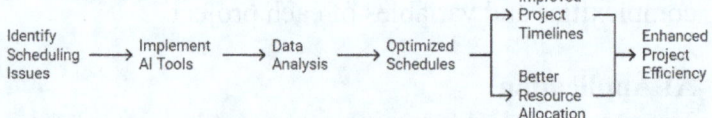

- Case Study 2: AI in Risk Management for a Large Construction Project

Background:
A global construction company managing a large multi-phase construction project faced challenges in identifying and managing potential risks. Environmental changes, supply chain delays, and safety-related risks posed significant threats to project success.

AI Application:
The company adopted an AI system to analyze vast amounts of project-related data, including environmental data, safety records, and supply chain information. The system used machine learning techniques to predict potential risks and assess their impact and likelihood.

Results:

- **Early Risk Identification:** The company was able to identify potential risks before they occurred, allowing for initiative-taking measures.
- **Reduced Delays:** Decreased delays caused by unforeseen risks by 25%.
- **Improved Safety:** The system helped identify potential safety hazards, leading to fewer incidents and increased compliance with safety standards.

Lessons Learned:

- **Predictive Analytics:** AI can analyze large datasets to forecast potential risks.

- **Data-Driven Decision Making:** AI supports project managers in making informed decisions based on accurate insights.
- **Initiative-taking Planning:** Early risk detection allows for effective mitigation strategies.

How to manage risks in a large construction project?

Traditional Risk Management   **AI-Powered Risk Management**

Relies on historical data and expert judgment to identify and mitigate risks.

Uses machine learning algorithms to analyze real-time data and predict potential risks.

- Case Study 3: Using AI to Enhance Communication and Stakeholder Management in Software Development

Background:
A geographically distributed software development team struggled with effective communication due to time zone differences and cultural variances, resulting in project delays and misunderstandings.

AI Application:
AI-powered chatbots were implemented to facilitate real-time communication among team members. The bots provided instant updates, answered frequently asked questions, and assisted in scheduling meetings considering the different time zones.

Results:

- **Improved Communication:** Reduced the need for synchronous meetings by 30%, enhancing communication efficiency.
- **Increased Productivity:** The team could focus on core tasks without being distracted by repetitive inquiries.
- **Enhanced Stakeholder Satisfaction:** Provided timely, accurate information to stakeholders, increasing their confidence and satisfaction with the project.

Lessons Learned:

- **Facilitating Global Communication:** AI can bridge language and time zone barriers, improving collaboration among international teams.

- **Automating Support:** Continuous support for team members and stakeholders through automated responses.
- **Improving Stakeholder Management:** Effective communication channels enhance stakeholder satisfaction and trust.

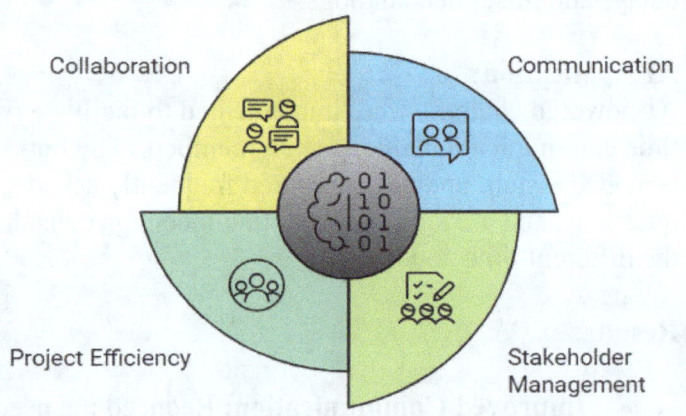

Conclusion:
These case studies demonstrate the positive impact of AI applications across various aspects of project management. By improving scheduling, risk management, and communication, companies have achieved increased efficiency, reduced costs, and enhanced project outcomes. This underscores the importance of adopting modern technologies and leveraging AI capabilities for success in today's competitive environments.

Sources:

- Case Studies 1 & 2: "How AI Is Revolutionizing Project Management: Three Use Cases" – Article by Peter Kestenholz, Forbes, 2023.
- Case Study 3: "Case Studies: Success Stories of AI in Project Management" – Article by Justin Underhill, LinkedIn, 2024.

13.2 Lessons Learned and Best Practices

- Analyzing **Key Success Factors:**

  - Focus on solving bona fide business problems rather than merely applying technology.
  - Ensure the quality and relevance of data used to train AI models.
  - Involve key stakeholders at all project stages.

- Importance **of Training and Skills Development:**

  - Develop comprehensive training programs to enhance team proficiency in AI technologies.
  - Foster a deep understanding of AI capabilities and limitations.
  - Encourage a culture of continuous learning and adaptability to modern technologies.

- Need **for a Clear Integration Strategy:**

  - Create a phased plan for applying AI in project management processes.
  - Identify priority application areas based on expected added value.
  - Ensure alignment with the organization's strategic objectives.

- Importance **of Transparency and Continuous Communication:**

  - Establish effective communication channels with all stakeholders.
  - Clarify how AI is being used and its impact on processes and outcomes.
  - Proactively address concerns and challenges.

13.3 ROI Analysis

- Quantifiable **Cost Savings and Productivity Increases:**

  - Thirty percent reduction in scheduling time using AI tools.
  - Twenty-five percent improvement in project estimate accuracy through predictive analytics.
  - Twenty percent decrease in project delays via enhanced risk management.

- Intangible **Benefits:**

  - Improved decision quality through advanced data analysis.
  - Increased customer satisfaction from enhanced communication and expectation management.
  - Strengthened organizational ability to innovate and adapt to market changes.

- Cost-Benefit Analysis:

  - Compare the costs of implementing and maintaining AI systems against realized savings.

- Evaluate indirect costs, such as training and change management.
- Consider long-term benefits, such as improved competitiveness.

It is important to note that these examples and figures may vary across different organizations and projects, and a thorough analysis should be performed for each case to determine the actual ROI.

Chapter 14: The Future of Project Management with Artificial Intelligence

14.1 Emerging Trends and New Technologies

- Deep Learning and Its Applications in Big Data Analysis for Projects:

  - Deep learning can analyze vast amounts of project data more swiftly and efficiently than traditional methods.
  - Utilizing deep neural networks to uncover complex patterns in project data and predict future outcomes.
  - Applications include predicting project delays, optimizing resource allocation, and accurately identifying potential risks.

- Advanced Robotics and Process Automation in Project Management:

  - Smart robots can automate routine tasks such as data collection and reporting.
  - Development of bots to assist project managers with administrative and analytical tasks.
  - Automating project monitoring and control processes using intelligent systems.

- Augmented Reality and Virtual Reality in Project Visualization and Planning:

  - Using augmented reality to visualize projects in their real-world environments before execution.
  - Applying virtual reality in training project teams and simulating various scenarios.

- Enhancing collaboration among geographically distributed team members using shared virtual environments.

- Quantum Computing and Its Impact on Solving Complex Project Problems:

  - Utilizing quantum computing power to address complex optimization problems in project management.
  - Developing quantum algorithms to improve project scheduling and resource allocation more efficiently.
  - Addressing security and encryption issues in sensitive projects using quantum techniques.

14.2 The Evolving Role of the Project Manager

- Transitioning from Traditional Tasks to Strategic and Creative Roles:

  - Project managers will focus on strategic planning and complex decision-making rather than routine tasks.
  - Increased emphasis on innovation and finding creative solutions to unforeseen challenges.
  - Development of transformational leadership skills to motivate teams and manage change in a dynamic work environment.

- Importance of Developing Skills in AI and Data Science:

  - Understanding the fundamentals of AI and its applications in project management is essential.

- Developing data analysis skills and using advanced analytical tools.
- Learning how to integrate AI technologies into project management processes.

• Project Manager as a Translator Between Technical Teams and Stakeholders:

- Ability to translate complex technical concepts into language understood by non-technical stakeholders.
- Facilitating effective communication between AI development teams and business units.
- Ensuring that AI solutions align with project objectives and stakeholder needs.

• Increased Focus on Human Aspects and Effective Leadership in the Age of Automation:

- Developing emotional intelligence and empathy to handle human challenges in automated work environments.
- Focusing on building trust and motivating teams amid increasing reliance on technology.
- Managing the tension between automation and the need for human interaction in projects.

14.3 Future Challenges and Opportunities

• Addressing Ethical and Legal Issues Related to AI Use:

- Ensuring transparency and accountability in using AI systems for decision-making.
- Addressing privacy and data protection issues in AI-dependent projects.

- Developing an ethical framework for using AI in project management.

- Enhancing Human-Machine Collaboration in the Workplace:

  - Designing processes and systems that allow seamless interaction between humans and intelligent systems.
  - Developing skills for collaboration with smart systems to achieve optimal results.
  - Redesigning project team roles and responsibilities to fit hybrid work environments.

- Tackling Cybersecurity Challenges and Data Protection in AI-Driven Projects:

  - Developing advanced security strategies to protect data and intelligent systems from cyber threats.
  - Ensuring the integrity and reliability of data used in training and operating AI systems.
  - Addressing new security risks arising from the use of advanced AI technologies.

- Exploring New Opportunities to Enhance Project Management Efficiency and Effectiveness Using Emerging Technologies:

  - Using AI technologies to improve decision-making processes and risk management in complex projects.
  - Developing advanced predictive models to enhance cost estimation and project scheduling.

- Exploring new applications of emerging technologies such as IoT and blockchain in project management.

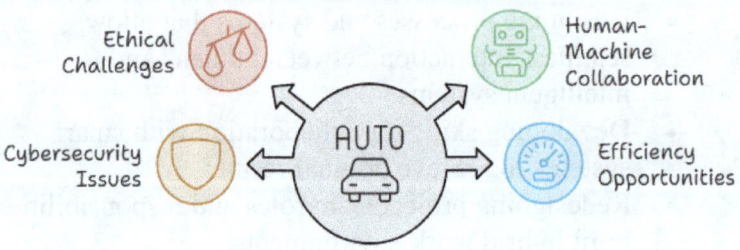

Future of Project Management with AI

By understanding and embracing these emerging trends and technologies, project managers can better prepare for future challenges and opportunities in project management. This will require continuous skill and knowledge development, as well as the ability to adapt to rapid changes in technology and the work environment.

Chapter 15: Conclusion and Recommendations

15.1 Summary of Key Points

- The Importance of AI in Transforming Project Management Practices:

  - AI automates routine tasks, allowing project managers to focus on strategic aspects.
  - It analyzes vast amounts of data swiftly and efficiently to extract valuable insights.
  - Enhances the ability to predict potential risks and challenges in projects.

- Positive Impact on Efficiency and Decision-Making Accuracy:

  - Provides precise analytics that support data-driven decision-making.
  - Improves the accuracy of cost and schedule estimates.
  - Helps identify optimal courses of action based on scenario analysis.

- AI's Role in Enhancing Organizational Competitiveness:

  - Empowers organizations to respond quickly to market changes and adapt to evolving conditions.
  - Improves product and service quality through advanced analysis and process optimization.
  - Assists in reducing costs and increasing productivity, thereby enhancing competitive advantage.

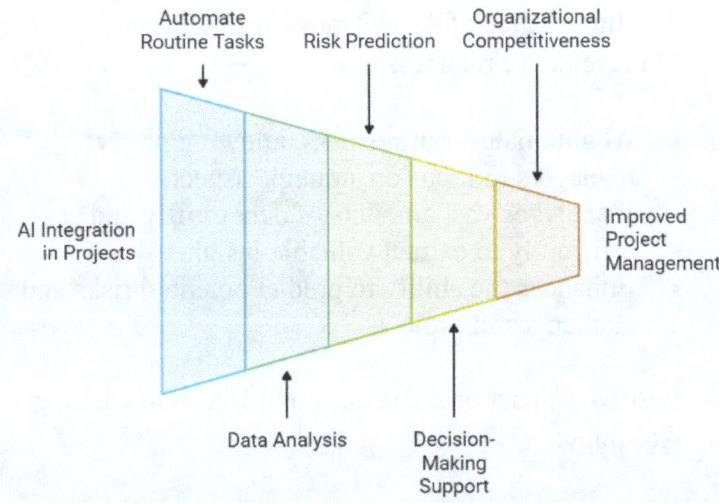

15.2 Recommendations for Project Managers and Organizations

- Invest in Continuous Training and Development in AI:

  - Develop comprehensive training programs to enhance team skills in AI technologies.
  - Encourage continuous learning and adaptation to new developments in AI.
  - Foster an organizational culture that supports innovation and experimentation with AI technologies.

- Adopt a Gradual Approach to AI Implementation:

  - Start with small, manageable projects to gain experience and build confidence.

- Gradually scale AI usage as experience and success increase.
- Continuously evaluate results and adjust strategies accordingly.

- Develop Change Management Strategies to Ensure Employee Acceptance of New Technologies:

  - Communicate clearly about the benefits and impacts of AI on daily operations.
  - Involve employees in the transformation process and encourage their participation in developing AI solutions.
  - Provide necessary support and resources to help employees adapt to changes.

- Focus on Ethical Considerations and Transparency in AI Use:

  - Establish a clear ethical framework for using AI in project management.
  - Ensure transparency in how data is used, and decisions are made by AI systems.
  - Consider the social and ethical implications of AI applications and mitigate potential negative impacts.

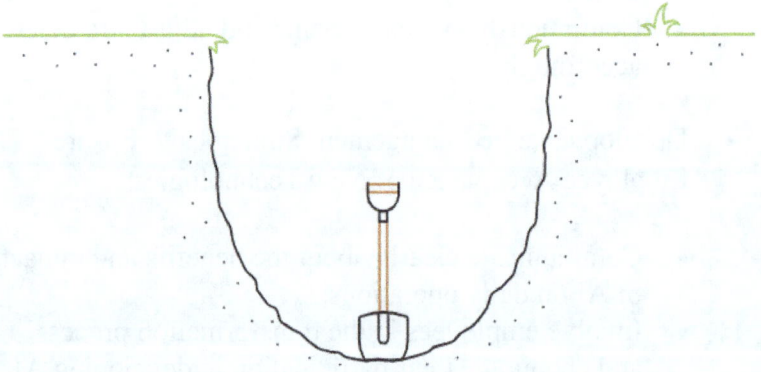
Lack of acceptance hinders effective AI implementation.

15.3 Next Steps for Adopting AI in Project Management

- Conduct a Comprehensive Assessment of Organizational Readiness for AI Adoption:

  - Evaluate the current technological infrastructure and its suitability for AI applications.
  - Analyze the existing skills and capabilities of employees in AI.
  - Identify gaps and needs for successful AI implementation.

- Identify Priority Areas for AI Application:

  - Analyze current processes and tasks to determine where AI can have the greatest impact.
  - Focus on projects that offer rapid and tangible value to the organization.

- Develop a plan for gradually expanding AI applications across various aspects of project management.

- Create a Specialized Team to Lead AI Initiatives in Project Management:

    - Form a multidisciplinary team combining AI experts and experienced project managers.
    - Define clear roles and responsibilities for team members.
    - Provide the necessary resources and support for the team's success.

- Develop a Long-Term Plan for Integrating AI Across All Aspects of Project Management:

    - Create an unobstructed vision for how AI will be utilized in project management in the long term.
    - Set measurable goals and milestones to track progress.
    - Regularly review and update the plan to reflect technological advancements and changes in organizational needs.

Steps to AI Integration in Project Management

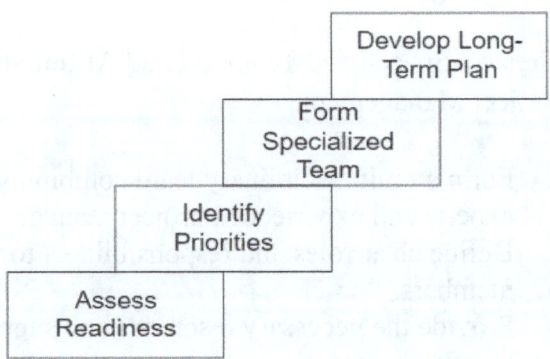

15.4 Final Thoughts

- Reinforcing that AI is a Tool to Enhance Project Managers' Capabilities, Not Replace Them:

    - AI acts as a powerful assistant to project managers, enhancing their capabilities and enabling better decision-making.
    - Human judgment and experience remain essential, especially in complex situations requiring creative thinking and emotional intelligence.

- Emphasizing the Need for Balance Between Technology and the Human Element in Project Management:

    - Combining the power of AI with unique human skills can lead to exceptional outcomes.
    - Continuous development of human skills alongside technological advancement is necessary.

- Call for Ongoing Research and Innovation in AI Applications in Project Management:

  - Encourage the continuous exploration of new AI applications in project management.
  - Invite the professional community to engage in developing best practices and sharing experiences.
  - Emphasize the importance of collaboration between industry and academia to drive innovation in this field.

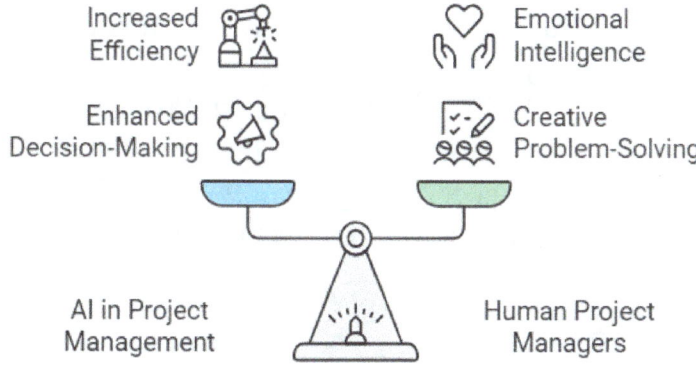

Balancing AI and Human Skills in Project Management

Chapter 16: Sources

In this chapter, we will present a list of the sources that were used in this study. These sources include books, references, articles, case studies, and other electronic resources utilized in research and analysis.

Books:

- 1. "Project Management: The Managerial Process" by Erik W. Larson and Clifford F. Gray
- 2. "Artificial Intelligence in Project Management" by Dr. Ahmed El-Sawy
- 3. "Project Management with Artificial Intelligence" by Dr. John R. Turner
-

References:

- 1. "A Guide to the Project Management Body of Knowledge (PMBOK Guide)" by Project Management Institute (PMI)
- 2. "Artificial Intelligence in Project Management: A Systematic Review" by International Journal of Project Management
- 3. "The Future of Project Management: Trends, Opportunities, and Challenges" by Project Management Journal
-

Articles:

- 1. "How AI Is Revolutionizing Project Management" by Forbes
- 2. "The Role of Artificial Intelligence in Project Management" by Harvard Business Review
- 3. "AI in Project Management: Benefits, Challenges, and Future Directions" by Journal of Management and Organization
-

Case Studies:

- 1. "Case Study: Using AI in Project Management at NASA" by NASA
- 2. "Case Study: AI-Powered Project Management at Google" by Google
- 3. "Case Study: Artificial Intelligence in Project Management at Microsoft" by Microsoft

Electronic Resources:

- 1. Project Management Institute (PMI) - https://www.pmi.org/
- 2. International Journal of Project Management - https://www.journals.elsevier.com/international-journal-of-project-management/
- 3. Harvard Business Review - https://hbr.org/

- 4. Forbes - https://www.forbes.com/
- 5. NASA - https://www.nasa.gov/
- 6. Google - https://www.google.com/
- 7. Microsoft - https://www.microsoft.com/

www.ingramcontent.com/pod-product-compliance
Lightning Source LLC
Chambersburg PA
CBHW051535240526
45471CB00020B/2675